WHAT'S MY RULE?

By

Dave Logothetti
University of Santa Clara

and

Teddy Logothetti
San Lorenzo Valley Intermediate School

DALE SEYMOUR PUBLICATIONS
Pearson Learning Group

Editors: Lyn Savage, Geri Rothacker
Production Coordinator: Ruth Cottrell
Illustrator: Margaret Sanfilippo

This book is dedicated to our friend, George Pólya.

ISBN 0-86651-106-7
United States of America
14 15 16 17 18   07 06 05 04 03

Dale
Seymour
Publications

Pearson Learning Group

1-800-321-3106
www.pearsonlearning.com

CONTENTS

PREFACE

The purpose of this book is to provide pleasant guessing activities that introduce middle-grade and beginning high school students to various algebraic functions: linear functions such as $n \rightarrow 7n + 2$, and exponential functions such as $n \rightarrow n^3$ or $n \rightarrow 3^n$. The vehicles for this introduction are problem-solving situations based on the questions What's my rule? or What comes out? or What comes next? We have found that oral work based on these questions invariably captures the attention of a class, if it is not overdone so that it becomes too routine. This has been true for children as young as first graders and for mature students at the college level.

We want to thank Dale Seymour, Lyn Savage, Jonathan Logothetti, and Vincent Logothetti for their help with the ideas in this book.

D.L. and T.L.
Gold Gulch, Felton, California
February, 1982

TEACHING SUGGESTIONS

First of all, we suggest that teachers, unlike students using this book, turn to the section "How to Discover Rules." By reading this section and familiarizing yourself with the arithmetic patterns that are used here, you will know some of the inside secrets that the students will discover for themselves in the activities. Then, having done your homework, you'll be ready for the fun of conducting stimulating lessons.

Presenting the Activities

Perhaps the most dynamic and entertaining way to use this book is as an informal script for conversations between you and your students. For example, you might show one of the "What's My Rule?" activities, with 4 going in one ear and 13 coming out the other. Ask, "What number do you think will come out if 10 goes in?" The students will probably offer several guesses before they come up with the answer that you have in mind (31). This variety of guesses tends to commit the students to solving the problem. If no student suggests the answer you have in mind, tell the class that the answer you were thinking of was 31. Then ask, "What number do you think will come out if 2 goes in?" Continue accepting guesses and asking more questions. Eventually some student will say, "Oh! I get it! Ask me another number." If you give a fairly large number such as 100, and if the excited student gives back 301, you'll know that the student has found the rule "multiply by 3 and add 1." Depending on the mathematical level of the class, you might go on to ask, "What comes out if n goes in?" It is quite likely that any student who can answer the question for 100 has understood the rule, whether or not it is expressed as the function $n \rightarrow 3n + 1$.

With crafty interrogation on your part, this question-and-answer, trial-and-error type of lesson can become almost completely nonthreatening for the students. Suppose a student answers "24" while you are waiting for "34." Instead of labeling the answer "incorrect," you might ask how the student arrived at 24, or ask the student to look at a sequence of answers that lead up to 34. Perhaps best of all, you might ask another question to which 24 really is the desired answer. The chances are that when asked this type of question, the student will catch the error and correct it without someone else drawing it explicitly to the attention of the world. Thus the student gains in understanding without suffering any bruise to the ego.

Other ways to use this book are variations on this conversational method of brainstorming with the whole class. One variation is for small groups of students to work with the problems, taking turns filling the teacher's role of holding the book and asking questions of the others. The first student to discover the idea of the rule might then take the teacher's role and present the next problem, and so forth. Another variation is to reproduce the pages and give them to students for individual work.

In an effort to maintain the feeling of person-to-person oral work, we have arranged the answers to the questions so that a student may, if baffled, look up one answer without accidentally seeing all of the rest of the answers for the page with which he or she is struggling. If you choose to have the students work individually, we suggest that you also reproduce the Answer List pages and either put them in clear plastic sleeves or laminate them for durability.

Extending the Activities

For more originality, we have included some blank versions of our favorite pages. These can be used by either you or your students to create more problems using different rules. You might post copies of the blank pages on a bulletin board as an ongoing challenge. One student could present the first three clues, and the rest of the class could try to guess the answers to the remaining questions on the page. The first student to discover the rule would then invent the next problem to challenge the class, and so on. You can make a blank page from any of the activity pages by pasting pieces of white paper over the numerals printed there, and then copying the page.

Sequencing the Activities

The section "Not As Easy As 1, 2, 3" explains to students the nature of the problems in this book, noting that each problem is really a little guessing game that may have many correct answers. The challenge lies in guessing the answer that we, the authors, happen to have in mind. Meanwhile, there is no stigma attached to guessing answers other than those that we happen to have in our minds. You may want to use this section as the basis for a class discussion prior to beginning any of the activities. Older students might simply read this section on their own before beginning the "What's My Rule?" activities.

The section "How to Discover Rules" is written both for you and for your students. You may want to allow students to read parts of this section whenever they are stuck on a particular activity page. The more talented students might enjoy solving all the "What's My Rule?" and "What Comes Out?" activity pages on their own before reading this section.

Here they will see the ideas that they already have been using expressed explicitly. All students should read this section before tackling the activities titled "What Comes Next?"

The first set of activity pages for the students is titled "What's My Rule?" These pages consist of problems for which the answers are all linear functions, that is, of the form $n \rightarrow an + b$, where a and b are integers. For example, $n \rightarrow 4n + 3$, $n \rightarrow 4n - 3$, and $n \rightarrow 300 - 4n$ are linear functions. The activities are carefully sequenced, starting with simple additions such as $n \rightarrow n + 4$, passing through multiples such as $n \rightarrow 3n$, and culminating in relatively difficult subtractions of multiples from constants such as $n \rightarrow 300 - 4n$. At the end of this set of activity pages are review problems in which the problems are mixed together without any suggestive sequencing. The general pattern for each activity page is given on Answer List 4.

The activities titled "What Comes Out?" are similar to the "What's My Rule?" activities, except that they introduce exponential functions such as $n \rightarrow 3^n$ and $n \rightarrow n^3$. A few problems involving linear functions are included, just to keep the students on their toes. The last page in this section contains review problems.

The third set of activities is titled "What Comes Next?" These activities call for guessing the nth term of a sequence that uses either a linear or exponential function as described in "How to Discover Rules" and used in the previous activities. Generally, these problems tend to be more difficult than those in the earlier activities. Hence, these final activities offer a chance for students to apply what they've learned.

A Final Thought

Working with this book is meant to be fun. It is not fun to be constantly frustrated, never guessing the "right" answer. So when working with beginners or others whose mathematical egos are only in the tender, embryonic stages, please be prepared to accept answers that are consistent with the previous clues, even if they are not the answers that you have been seeking. (See "Not As Easy As 1, 2, 3" about the possibility of an infinite number of "correct" answers.) It would be not at all out of place to praise an unexpected, but consistent, answer more lavishly than the expected answer. Please look for good thinking on the part of the students, rather than for their mistakes. We have written this little book on the premise that it is fun to think, and even more fun to be praised for thinking. We hope that both you and your students will have fun with this book, and with the questions and answers that it stimulates.

NOT AS EASY AS 1,2,3

This book is full of problems, or puzzles if you prefer, in the form of guessing games. For each problem we will give you some samples of numbers going in and numbers coming out. For example, in Activity 1 we tell you 3 goes in and 7 comes out, 8 goes in and 12 comes out, 2 goes in and 6 comes out. Then we give you some numbers going in, and you are supposed to guess the numbers that come out. In Activity 1 we tell you that 11 goes in and ask what number comes out.

All of this sounds very simple, but it may be trickier than you think. The reason for this trickiness is that for each problem there are an infinite number of "correct" answers! Think about the following:

    1 goes in and 1 comes out.

    2 goes in and 2 comes out.

    3 goes in and 3 comes out.

    If 4 goes in, what comes out?

The problem here is that you are supposed to read our minds and guess what we are thinking of. (Right now you might put this book aside and try to think of numbers that might reasonably come out when 4 goes in.)

What might we be thinking? Well, of course we might be thinking that if 4 goes in, then 4 comes out. If so, that wouldn't make a very interesting mystery. Here are some other ideas of what we might be thinking:

    IDEA 1: 1 goes in; 1 comes out.

                  2 goes in; 2 comes out.

                  3 goes in; $1 + 2 = 3$ comes out.

                  4 goes in; $2 + 3 = 5$ comes out.

                  5 goes in; $3 + 5 = 8$ comes out.

                  If this were what we were thinking, we'd be thinking of *Fibonacci numbers* where each number is found by adding the two that came before.

    IDEA 2: 1 goes in; 1 comes out.

                  2 goes in; 2 comes out.

                  3 goes in; 3 comes out.

                  4 goes in; the remainder of $4 \div 3$, or 1 comes out.

                  5 goes in; the remainder of $5 \div 3$, or 2 comes out.

                  6 goes in; the remainder of $6 \div 3$, or 0 DOESN'T come out (because we want no zeros today), and 3 comes out instead.

                  7 goes in; 1 comes out.

                  8 goes in; 2 comes out.

                  9 goes in; 3 comes out.

                  And so on.

IDEA 3: 1 goes in; $(1 \times 1 \times 1) - (6 \times 0 \times 0) = 1$ comes out.
2 goes in; $(2 \times 2 \times 2) - (6 \times 1 \times 1) = 2$ comes out.
3 goes in; $(3 \times 3 \times 3) - (6 \times 2 \times 2) = 3$ comes out.
4 goes in; $(4 \times 4 \times 4) - (6 \times 3 \times 3) = 10$ comes out.
5 goes in; $(5 \times 5 \times 5) - (6 \times 4 \times 4) = 29$ comes out.
If this were what we were thinking, we'd be rather tricky, which we sometimes are!

IDEA 4: 1 goes in; $(2) - (0 \times 0) - 1 = 1$ comes out.
2 goes in; $(2 \times 2) - (1 \times 1) - 1 = 2$ comes out.
3 goes in; $(2 \times 2 \times 2) - (2 \times 2) - 1 = 3$ comes out.
4 goes in; $(2 \times 2 \times 2 \times 2) - (3 \times 3) - 1 = 6$ comes out.
5 goes in; $(2 \times 2 \times 2 \times 2 \times 2) - (4 \times 4) - 1 = 15$ comes out.
More trickiness!

IDEA 5: 1 goes in; 1 comes out.
2 goes in; $(1 \times 2) \div 1 = 2$ comes out.
3 goes in; $(1 \times 2 \times 3) \div 2 = 3$ comes out.
4 goes in; $(1 \times 2 \times 3 \times 4) \div 3 = 8$ comes out.
5 goes in; $(1 \times 2 \times 3 \times 4 \times 5) \div 8 = 15$ comes out.
This *is* what we were thinking.

Well, we could go on and on. The point is that there are an infinite number of rules that would tell us that if 1 goes in then 1 comes out; if 2 goes in then 2 comes out; if 3 goes in then 3 comes out.

You might say, "YOW! I'll never be able to guess the rules these guys make up." Ah, but you see we are nice guys, and most of our rules involve just simple addition, subtraction, and multiplication. You'll see when you start trying the problems.

Trying, by the way, is the most important part of using this book. The answers are not nearly as important as the process of guessing that you use in trying to find our mystery numbers. That's one of the reasons that in the "What's My Rule?" activities, we use numbers going in one ear and out the other. "In one ear and out the other" means not remembering what you've heard. In all the activities we hope that you do not concentrate on the answers and try to memorize them, but that you do try to remember how you think when you do your arithmetic detective work. That is, don't try to remember answers as much as you try to remember the tricks we use. And if you don't happen to guess our trick, don't feel badly about it. Remember, there are many, many correct answers, and the ones that you think of may be better than ours, even if we don't list them in the Answers section at the back of the book.

Now go have some fun doing mathematical detective work!

6

HOW TO DISCOVER RULES

In this section we will suggest some ways to discover rules. You must remember, though, that these suggestions are only ideas that *might* work. Because there are an infinite number of correct answers for every rule-discovering situation, you are really just guessing which rule we have in mind. Therefore, you cannot count on our suggestions to always help you find our rule.

Looking at Differences

If you cannot see a number pattern right away, you might look at the differences between the "out" numbers and compare them with the differences between the "in" numbers. This is perhaps the most natural way to do detective work with numbers. Let's look at some examples.

Example 1:

"In Numbers"	"Out Numbers"
3	8
4	9
8	13
14	?
n	??

Here the difference between 8 and 9 is 1, while the difference between 3 and 4 is also 1. The difference between 9 and 13 is 4, while the difference between 4 and 8 is also 4. Therefore, since the difference between 8 and 14 is 6, it is a good idea to guess that the difference between 13 and *?* is also 6, so that if 14 goes in, then $13 + 6 = 19$ comes out. You might also look at the differences between the pairs of "in numbers" and "out numbers": $8 - 3 = 5$; $9 - 4 = 5$; $13 - 8 = 5$; $19 - 14 = 5$. We, therefore, cleverly guess that if n goes in, then $n + 5$ comes out.

Example 2:

"In Numbers"	"Out Numbers"
9	81
18	72
25	65
30	?
n	??

The difference between 81 and 72 is 9 (really -9, if you know what that means), so the "out numbers" are going down by 9; meanwhile, the difference between 9 and 18 is also 9. This makes us suspect that if the "in numbers" go up by 1, then the "out numbers" go down by 1; if the "in numbers" go up by 2, then the "out numbers" go down by 2; and so on. The difference between 18 and 25 is 7, while the difference between 72 and 65 is a downward 7, which fits in with what we suspect. Therefore, since the difference between 25 and 30 is 5, we expect that the difference between 65 and ? will be a downward 5, and so if 30 goes in, then $65 - 5 = 60$ comes out. Now if the "in numbers" go up by the same amount that the "out numbers" go down, then the sum of any pair of "in" and "out" numbers must stay the same: $9 + 81 = 90$; $18 + 72 = 90$; $25 + 65 = 90$; $30 + 60 = 90$. We, therefore, guess that if n goes in, then $90 - n$ comes out.

Example 3:

"In Numbers"	"Out Numbers"
4	2
6	6
10	14
20	?
n	??

The difference between 4 and 6 is 2, while the difference between 2 and 6 is 4; the difference between 6 and 10 is 4, while the difference between 6 and 14 is 8. Ho! It appears that if the "in numbers" go up by a certain amount, then the "out numbers" go up by twice that amount. So if the difference between 10 and 20 is 10, then the difference between 14 and ? will be 20, so ? $= 14 + 20 = 34$. Also, since the "out differences" are always 2 times the "in differences," we suspect that if n goes in, then some number related to $2n$ comes out. Let's go back and look at the clues again.

"In Number" = n	$2n$	"Out Number"
4	8	2
6	12	6
10	20	14
20	40	?

Notice that the difference between 8 and 2 is 6, between 12 and 6 is 6, between 20 and 14 is 6. We, therefore, strongly suspect that the difference between 40 and ? is also 6, so that ? $= 40 - 6 = 34$. And we also guess that if n goes in, then $2n - 6$ comes out. TA DA!

Example 4:

"In Numbers"	"Out Numbers"
2	26
5	20
9	12
11	?
n	??

The difference between 2 and 5 is 3, while the difference between 26 and 20 is a downward 6 (alias -6). The difference between 5 and 9 is 4, while the difference between 20 and 12 is a downward 8. Therefore, we suspect that if the difference between 9 and 11 is 2, the difference between 12 and ? will be a downward 4. So we guess that ? $= 12 - 4 = 8$. Let's look at the clues again.

8

"In Numbers" = n	$2n$	"Out Numbers"
2	4	26
5	10	20
9	18	12
11	22	8

If we look at these clues a long time, we notice that $4 + 26 = 30$, $10 + 20 = 30$, $18 + 12 = 30$, and $22 + 8 = 30$. This makes us suspect that $2n + ?? = 30$, so *??* must be $30 - 2n$. TA DA!

Example 5:

"In Numbers"	"Out Numbers"
3	13
5	5
6	1
2	?
n	??

The difference between 3 and 5 is 2; the difference between 13 and 5 is a downward 8. The difference between 5 and 6 is 1; the difference between 5 and 1 is a downward 4. So the downward differences appear to be divisible by 4. Let's look at the clues again, this time putting in multiples of 4.

"In Numbers" = n	$4n$	"Out Numbers"
3	12	13
5	20	5
6	24	1
2	8	?

We notice that $12 + 13 = 25$; $20 + 5 = 25$; $24 + 1 = 25$. So $8 + ?$ probably is 25. So $? = 17$. Therefore, it appears that $4n + ?? = 25$, so $?? = 25 - 4n$. TA DA!

Looking at Quotients

If you can see no good patterns in looking at the differences between the "out numbers," you might try looking at the quotients that result from the division of one "out number" by another.

Example 6:

"In Numbers"	"Out Numbers"
1	6
3	54
4	162
2	?
n	??

Let's look at 54 divided by 6; this is $9 = 3^2$. Meanwhile, the difference between 1 and 3 is 2. 162 divided by 54 is $3 = 3^1$; the difference between 3 and 4 is 1. Now the difference between 1 and 2 is 1; therefore, we expect the quotient of *?* divided by 6 to be $3^1 = 3$, so that *?* is 3 times 6 or 18. We seem to have a rule of 3 here.

"In Numbers"	"Out Numbers"
1	$6 = 2 \times 3^1$
3	$54 = 2 \times 3^3$
4	$162 = 2 \times 3^4$
2	$18 = 2 \times 3^2$
n	??

So we think the "out number" for n should be 2×3^n. TA DA!

Example 7:

"In Numbers"	"Out Numbers"
2	4
3	8
5	32
8	?
n	??

The difference between 2 and 3 is 1; and to go from 4 to 8, we multiply by $2 = 2^1$. The difference between 3 and 5 is 2; and to go from 8 to 32, we multiply by $4 = 2^2$. The difference between 5 and 8 is 3; and to go from 32 to ?, we seem to need to multiply by $2^3 = 8$, so that ? turns out to be $32 \times 8 = 256$. Let's look at the clues again.

"In Numbers"	"Out Numbers"
2	$4 = 2^2$
3	$8 = 2^3$
5	$32 = 2^5$
8	$256 = 2^8$
n	??

So, we cleverly guess that when n goes in, 2^n comes out.

Example 8:

"In Numbers"	"Out Numbers"
2	14
4	86
5	248
3	?
n	??

The difference between 2 and 4 is 2, while the difference between 14 and 86 is 72. The difference between 4 and 5 is 1, while the difference between 86 and 248 is 162. The difference between 2 and 5 is 3, while the difference between 14 and 248 is 234. What do 72, 162, and 234 have in common? Well, they are all divisible by 3. So, let's go back to the original clues, looking for 3s.

"In Numbers"	"Out Numbers"
2	$14 = 3^2 + 5$
4	$86 = 3^4 + 5$
5	$248 = 3^5 + 5$
3	?

So, we guess that if 3 goes in, then $3^3 + 5 = 32$ comes out, and if n goes in, then $3^n + 5$ comes out. TA DA!

10

Recognizing Famous Numbers

The last examples depend on our recognizing certain famous numbers. Here are some lists of numbers that may help you find patterns and rules.

Odd Numbers. $1,3,5,7,9,11,13,15,17,19,21,23,\ldots,(2n-1),\ldots$
(That expression involving n means that an odd number is just 1 less than some even number.)

Even Numbers, or Multiples of 2. $2,4,6,8,10,12,14,\ldots,2n,\ldots$

Multiples of 3. $3,6,9,12,15,18,21,24,27,30,33,36,39,42,\ldots,3n,\ldots$
(We know that you know these, but maybe you don't recognize them beyond $3 \times 12 = 36$. Notice that for all multiples of 3, the sum of the digits is also a multiple of 3.)

Multiples of 4. $4,8,12,16,20,\ldots,124,128,132,136,\ldots,4n,\ldots$
(The last 2 digits are always multiples of 4.)

Multiples of 5. $5,10,15,20,25,30,35,40,\ldots,5n,\ldots$
(The last digit is either 5 or 0.)

Multiples of 6. $6,12,18,24,30,36,42,\ldots,6n,\ldots$
(These are all even. Also, the sum of the digits is always a multiple of 3.)

Multiples of 8. $8,16,24,32,40,\ldots,1104,1112,1120,\ldots,8n,\ldots$
(The last 4 digits are always a multiple of 8.)

Multiples of 9. $9,18,27,36,45,54,63,72,\ldots,9n,\ldots$
(The sum of the digits is always a multiple of 9.)

Multiples of 11. $11,22,33,44,55,66,77,88,99,110,121,\ldots,11n,\ldots$
(If we add every other digit in each case, we get either the sum of the remaining digits or that sum plus a multiple of 11: for example, in 132, $1 + 2 = 3$; in 121, $1 + 1 = 2$; in 25740902, $2 + 7 + 0 + 0 = 5 + 4 + 9 + 2 + (-11)$.)

Note about differences between multiples: The difference between two multiples of 2 is also a multiple of 2. The difference between two multiples of 5 is also a multiple of 5, and so forth.

Powers of 2. Let's look at both the powers of 2 and their differences:

$$2^0 = 1$$
$$2^1 = 2$$
$$2^2 = 4$$
$$2^3 = 8$$
$$2^4 = 16$$
$$2^5 = 32$$
$$2^6 = 64$$
$$2^7 = 128$$
$$2^8 = 256$$
$$2^9 = 512$$
$$2^{10} = 1024$$

1
2
4
8
16
32
64
128
256
512

Powers of 3.

$$3^0 = 1$$
$$3^1 = 3$$
$$3^2 = 9$$
$$3^3 = 27$$
$$3^4 = 81$$
$$3^5 = 243$$
$$3^6 = 729$$
$$3^7 = 2187$$

2
6
18
54
162
486
1458

What's the interesting pattern in the differences?

Powers of 4.

$$4^0 = 1$$
$$4^1 = 4$$
$$4^2 = 16$$
$$4^3 = 64$$
$$4^4 = 256$$
$$4^5 = 1024$$

3
12
48
192
768

Where have we seen these powers before?

Powers of 5.

$$5^0 = 1$$
$$5^1 = 5$$
$$5^2 = 25$$
$$5^3 = 125$$
$$5^4 = 625$$
$$5^5 = 3125$$

4
20
100
500
2500

Powers of 6.

$$6^0 = 1$$
$$6^1 = 6$$
$$6^2 = 36$$
$$6^3 = 216$$
$$6^4 = 1296$$

5
30
180
1080

12

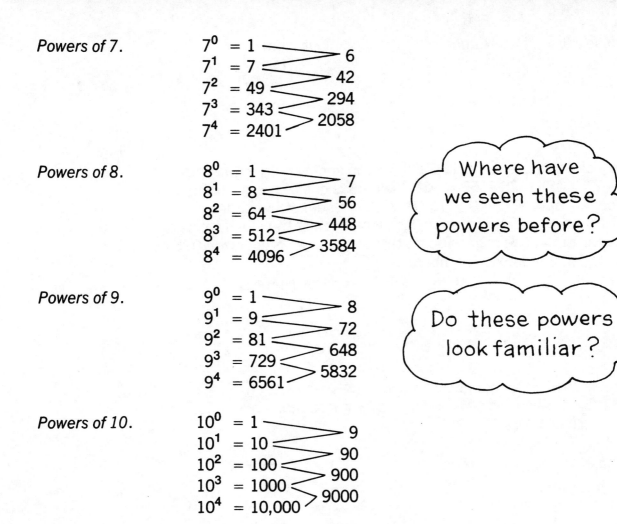

Powers of 7.

$$7^0 = 1$$
$$7^1 = 7$$
$$7^2 = 49$$
$$7^3 = 343$$
$$7^4 = 2401$$

6
42
294
2058

Powers of 8.

$$8^0 = 1$$
$$8^1 = 8$$
$$8^2 = 64$$
$$8^3 = 512$$
$$8^4 = 4096$$

7
56
448
3584

Powers of 9.

$$9^0 = 1$$
$$9^1 = 9$$
$$9^2 = 81$$
$$9^3 = 729$$
$$9^4 = 6561$$

8
72
648
5832

Powers of 10.

$$10^0 = 1$$
$$10^1 = 10$$
$$10^2 = 100$$
$$10^3 = 1000$$
$$10^4 = 10,000$$

9
90
900
9000

Where have we seen these powers before?

Do these powers look familiar?

Example 9:

"In Numbers"	"Out Numbers"
1	6
2	42
3	294
4	?
n	??

The "out numbers" are all multiples of 6 (since they are even and their digits add up to multiples of 3—for example, $2 + 9 + 4 = 15 = 5 \times 3$). Let's rewrite our clues and see what we can see.

"In Numbers"	"Out Numbers"
1	$6 = 6 \times 1 = 6 \times 7^0$
2	$42 = 6 \times 7 = 6 \times 7^1$
3	$294 = 6 \times 49 = 6 \times 7^2$
4	?

So, we craftily guess that if 4 goes in, then $6 \times 7^3 = 2058$ comes out. We also guess that if n goes in, then $6 \times 7^{n-1}$ comes out. TA DA!

Example 10:	"In Numbers"	"Out Numbers"
	2	17
	3	65
	5	1025
	4	?
	n	??

Let's look at differences and see if we can spot something familiar. $65 - 17 = 48$; $1025 - 65 = 960$. Well, 48 is one of the differences in the powers of 4, and $960 = 192 + 768$, the sum of two other differences of powers of 4. Therefore, let's look back at the clues, splitting off powers of 4. (We might also do this because we recognize 1025 as close to 1024, a famous number.)

"In Numbers"	"Out Numbers"
2	$17 = 4^2 + 1$
3	$65 = 4^3 + 1$
5	$1025 = 4^5 + 1$
4	?

It seems as if we should guess that when 4 goes in, then $4^4 + 1 = 256 + 1 = 257$ comes out. We might also guess that when n goes in, $4^n + 1$ comes out.

Example 11:	"In Numbers"	"Out Numbers"
	2	116
	4	104
	5	88
	6	?
	n	??

From 116 to 104 is a downward 12. From 104 to 88 is a downward 16. We may notice that 16 is a power of 2 and that $12 = 4 + 8$ is the sum of powers of 2. Since the differences are downward, we'd better think about subtraction as well as powers of 2. And we should also think about the "in numbers" as we look at the clues again.

"In Numbers"	"Out Numbers"
2	$116 = \text{Something} - 2^2 = 120 - 2^2$
4	$104 = \text{Something} - 2^4 = 120 - 2^4$
5	$88 = \text{Something} - 2^5 = 120 - 2^5$
6	?

Therefore, we guess that when 6 goes in, $120 - 2^6 = 120 - 64 = 56$ comes out. And we also guess that when n goes in, $120 - 2^n$ comes out. TA ultra-DA!

We can collect the same powers of different numbers to get some other famous families of numbers.

Squares, or
Second Powers.

$0^2 = 0$
$1^2 = 1$
$2^2 = 4$
$3^2 = 9$
$4^2 = 16$
$5^2 = 25$
$6^2 = 36$
$7^2 = 49$
$8^2 = 64$
$9^2 = 81$
$10^2 = 100$

1
3
5
7
9
11
13
15
17
19

Cubes, or
Third Powers.

$0^3 = 0$
$1^3 = 1$
$2^3 = 8$
$3^3 = 27$
$4^3 = 64$
$5^3 = 125$
$6^3 = 216$
$7^3 = 343$
$8^3 = 512$
$9^3 = 729$
$10^3 = 1000$

Fourth Powers.

$0^4 = 0$
$1^4 = 1$
$2^4 = 16$
$3^4 = 81$
$4^4 = 256$
$5^4 = 625$
$6^4 = 1296$

Fifth Powers.

$0^5 = 0$
$1^5 = 1$
$2^5 = 32$
$3^5 = 243$
$4^5 = 1024$

Sixth Powers.

$$0^6 = 0$$
$$1^6 = 1$$
$$2^6 = 64$$
$$3^6 = 729$$
$$4^6 = 4096$$

Example 12:

"In Numbers"	"Out Numbers"
3	82
4	257
1	2
2	?
n	??

We notice that the "out numbers" 82, 257, 2 look something like the famous numbers 81, 256, 1, (or 3^4, 4^4, 1^4). So we rewrite our clues.

"In Numbers"	"Out Numbers"
3	$82 = 3^4 + 1$
4	$257 = 4^4 + 1$
1	$2 = 1^4 + 1$
2	?

From this we guess that when 2 goes in, $2^4 + 1 = 17$ comes out. And it's just about as easy to guess that when n goes in, $2^n + 1$ comes out.

Example 13:

"In Numbers"	"Out Numbers"
1	4999
2	4936
3	4271
4	?
n	??

We see that the three "out numbers" are pretty close to 5000. Let's rewrite the clues.

"In Numbers"	"Out Numbers"
1	$4999 = 5000 - 1$
2	$4936 = 5000 - 64$
3	$4271 = 5000 - 729$
4	?

You may see that $1 = 1^6$, $64 = 2^6$, $729 = 3^6$. If so, your next guess is probably that if 4 goes in, then $5000 - 4^6 = 5000 - 4096 = 904$ comes out. Finally, for n going in, we guess that $5000 - n^6$ comes out. TA DA!

16

Clustering

Now that we have become acquainted with some famous numbers, we might try some clustering to guess the rules. With this method, if we don't recognize any numbers, we write several numbers clustered around the "out numbers" in hopes that some famous numbers will turn up.

Example 14:

"In Numbers"	"Out Numbers"
3	29
5	127
1	3
4	?
n	??

Pretend that you don't know where 29, 127, and 3 came from. Let's write some numbers clustered around those "out numbers."

"In Numbers"	"Out Clusters"
3	26,27,28,29,30,31,32
5	124,125,126,127,128,129,130
1	0,1,2,3,4,5,6

In the first cluster there are two famous numbers—$27 = 3^3$ and $32 = 2^5$. In the second cluster there may be only one famous number—$125 = 5^3$. In the third cluster there are lots of nice numbers, and we don't know which one to pick. That $125 = 5^3$ appears to be the best clue. The only number in the third cluster that is a cube is $1 = 1^3$. So let's look at the clues again.

"In Numbers"	"Out Numbers"
3	$29 = 3^3 + 2$
5	$127 = 5^3 + 2$
1	$3 = 1^3 + 2$
4	?

We guess that $? = 66 = 64 + 2 = 4^3 + 2$, and we also guess that when n goes in, $n^3 + 2$ comes out. TA DA!

Example 15:

"In Numbers"	"Out Numbers"
3	6
5	30
2	2
4	?
n	??

Let's rewrite with clusters.

"In Numbers"	"Out Clusters"
3	3,4,5,6,7,8,9
5	27,28,29,30,31,32,33
2	0,1,2,3,4,5

In the first cluster 4, 8, and 9 appear to be famous—$4 = 2^2$, $8 = 2^3$, and $9 = 3^2$. In the second cluster there are two famous numbers—$27 = 3^3$ and $32 = 2^5$. In the third cluster we might notice that $1 = 1^2 = 1^3 = 1^5 = 1^n = 2^0$, $2 = 2^1$, $3 = 3^1$, $4 = 2^2$. Which famous family is spread out through these three clusters? It might be powers of 2 or powers of 3. Which of these two families fits better with the "in numbers"? It seems to be the powers of 2.

"In Numbers"	"Out Numbers"
3	$6 = 2^3 - 2$
5	$30 = 2^5 - 2$
2	$2 = 2^2 - 2$
4	?

So we guess that if 4 goes in, then $2^4 - 2 = 16 - 2 = 14$ comes out. And if n goes in, then we think $2^n - 2$ comes out. TA DA!

A Final Comment

Successful guessing of rules depends on recognizing famous numbers. You can try to change unfamiliar numbers by adding, subtracting, multiplying, or dividing those numbers to, from, or by the same number. You can also get clues by finding differences, quotients, and sometimes sums of the "out numbers." If you still see nothing very attractive, you can look at clusters of numbers around the "out numbers." Good luck!

What's My Rule?

3 → → 7

8 → → 12   2 → → 6

Try to guess what number comes out. If you need a hint, look up the answer for **1** on Answer List 1, for **2** on Answer List 2, for **3** on Answer List 3, and for **4** on Answer list 4.

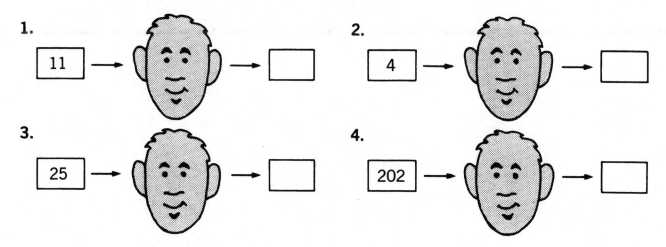

1.
11 → → ☐

2.
4 → → ☐

3.
25 → → ☐

4.
202 → → ☐

The answer to **4** is the number of bones in the human body.

What's My Rule?

Try to guess what number comes out. If you need a hint, look up the answer for **1** on Answer List 1, for **2** on Answer List 2, for **3** on Answer List 3, and for **4** on Answer list 4.

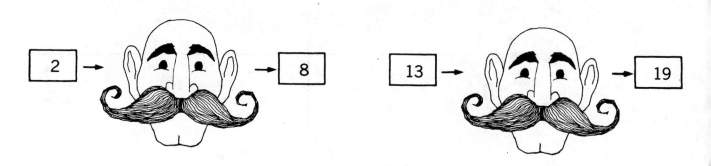

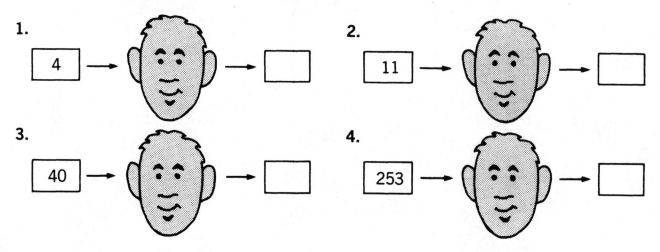

1.

2.

3.

4.

The answer to **4** is the length in centimeters of the longest recorded moustache.

20

What's My Rule?

Activity 3

2 → → 15

15 → → 28   8 → → 21

Try to guess what number comes out. If you need a hint, look up the answer for **1** on Answer List 1, for **2** on Answer List 2, for **3** on Answer List 3, and for **4** on Answer list 4.

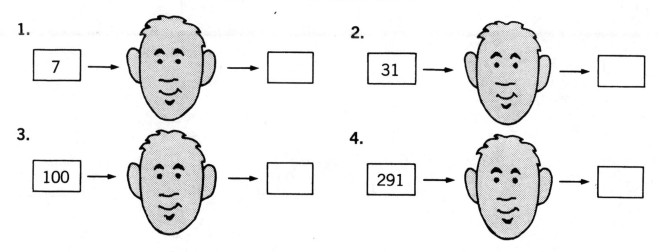

1.
7 → → ☐

2.
31 → → ☐

3.
100 → → ☐

4.
291 → → ☐

The answer to **4** is the weight in kilograms of the heaviest gorilla ever weighed.

What's My Rule?

How is this different from previous problems?

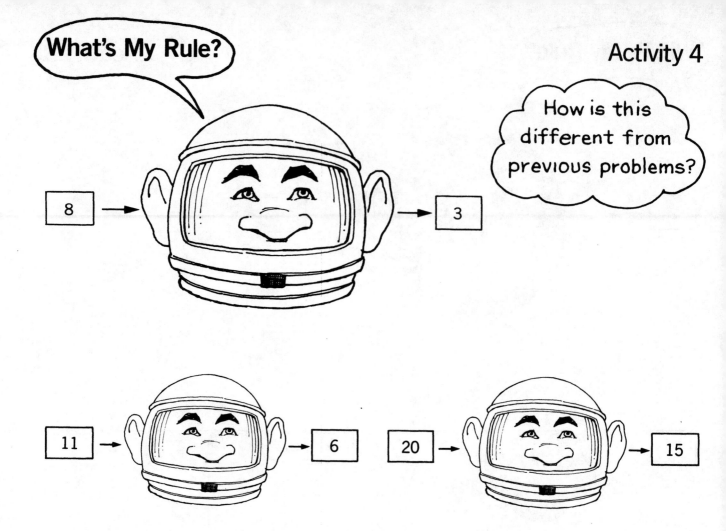

8 → 3

11 → 6

20 → 15

Try to guess what number comes out. If you need a hint, look up the answer for **1** on Answer List 1, for **2** on Answer List 2, for **3** on Answer List 3, and for **4** on Answer list 4.

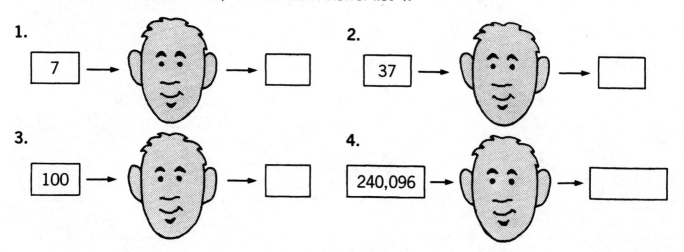

1. 7 →

2. 37 →

3. 100 →

4. 240,096 →

The answer to **4** is the speed in kilometers per hour of the fastest space vehicle.

22

What's My Rule?

20 → → 7

13 → → 0   23 → → 10

Try to guess what number comes out. If you need a hint, look up the answer for **1** on Answer List 1, for **2** on Answer List 2, for **3** on Answer List 3, and for **4** on Answer list 4.

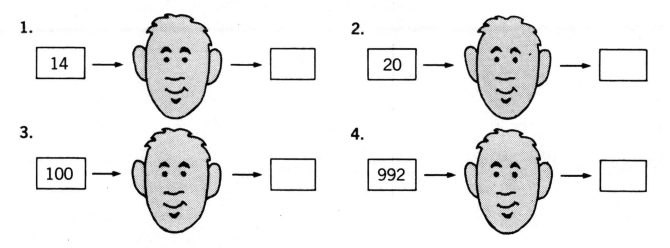

1. 14 →

2. 20 →

3. 100 →

4. 992 →

The answer to **4** is the height in meters of the world's highest waterfall.

What's My Rule?

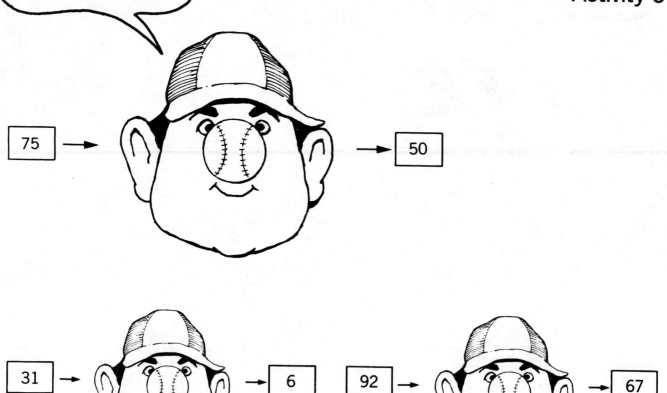

Try to guess what number comes out. If you need a hint, look up the answer for **1** on Answer List 1, for **2** on Answer List 2, for **3** on Answer List 3, and for **4** on Answer list 4.

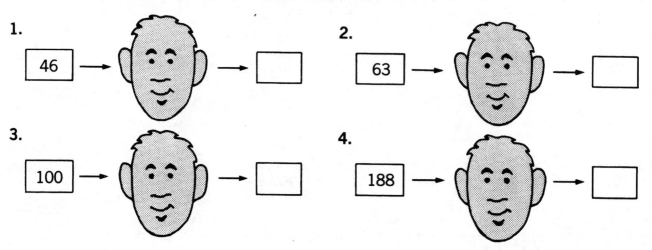

The answer to **4** is the speed in kilometers per hour of the fastest recorded pitch in baseball.

What's My Rule?

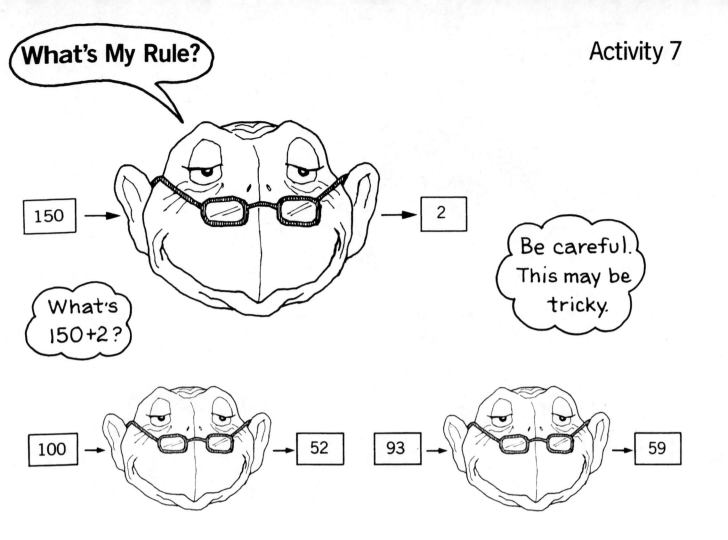

150 → 2

What's 150+2?

Be careful. This may be tricky.

100 → 52

93 → 59

Try to guess what number comes out. If you need a hint, look up the answer for **1** on Answer List 1, for **2** on Answer List 2, for **3** on Answer List 3, and for **4** on Answer list 4.

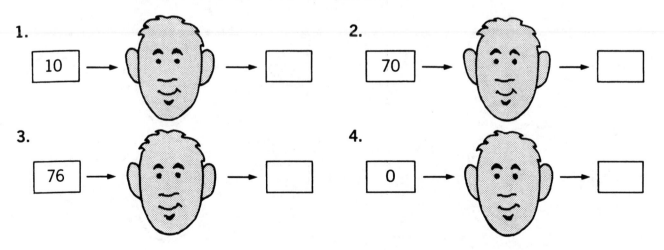

1. 10 →

2. 70 →

3. 76 →

4. 0 →

The answer to **4** is the oldest recorded age of any animal (a tortoise).

What's My Rule?

Activity 8

130 → [face] → 120

100 → [face] → 150   10 → [face] → 240

Try to guess what number comes out. If you need a hint, look up the answer for **1** on Answer List 1, for **2** on Answer List 2, for **3** on Answer List 3, and for **4** on Answer list 4.

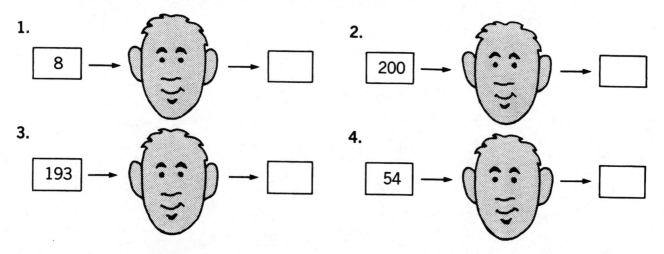

1. 8 → [face] → [ ]

2. 200 → [face] → [ ]

3. 193 → [face] → [ ]

4. 54 → [face] → [ ]

The answer to **4** is the weight in metric tons of the heaviest bell in the world.

26

What's My Rule?

163 → 37

98 → 102

3 → 197

Try to guess what number comes out. If you need a hint, look
up the answer for **1** on Answer List 1, for **2** on Answer List 2,
for **3** on Answer List 3, and for **4** on Answer list 4.

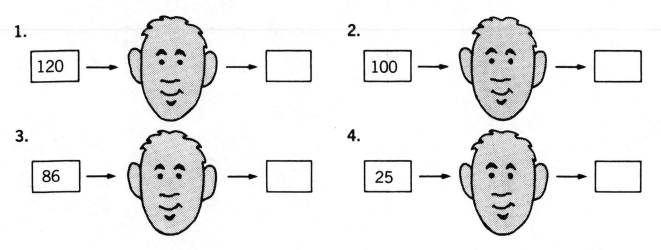

1. 120 →

2. 100 →

3. 86 →

4. 25 →

The answer to **4** is the number in thousands of the greatest
attendance at a concert.

What's My Rule?

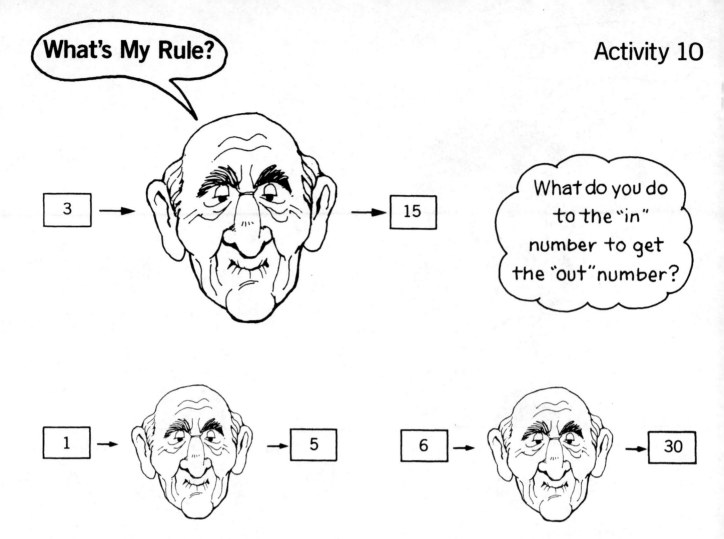

What do you do to the "in" number to get the "out" number?

3 → 15

1 → 5   6 → 30

Try to guess what number comes out. If you need a hint, look up the answer for **1** on Answer List 1, for **2** on Answer List 2, for **3** on Answer List 3, and for **4** on Answer list 4.

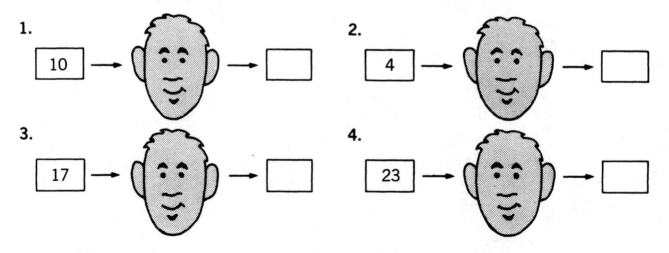

1. 10 →

2. 4 →

3. 17 →

4. 23 →

The answer to **4** is the age of the oldest man whose length of life was officially checked.

What's My Rule?

9 → 27

What kind of numbers do you get when you add up the digits of the "out" numbers?

14 → 42

27 → 81

Try to guess what number comes out. If you need a hint, look up the answer for **1** on Answer List 1, for **2** on Answer List 2, for **3** on Answer List 3, and for **4** on Answer list 4.

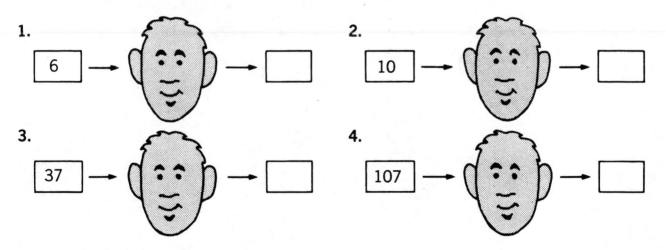

1. 6 → ☐

2. 10 → ☐

3. 37 → ☐

4. 107 → ☐

The answer to **4** is the height in meters of the world's highest bridge.

What's My Rule?

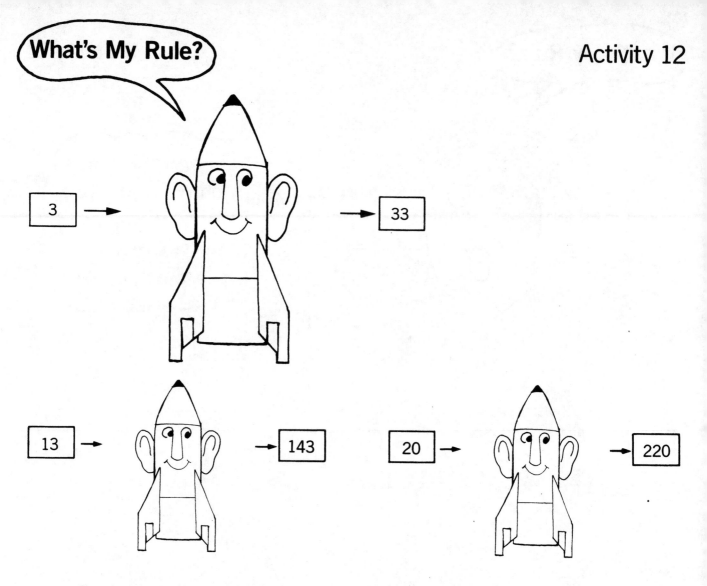

3 → 33

13 → 143

20 → 220

Try to guess what number comes out. If you need a hint, look up the answer for **1** on Answer List 1, for **2** on Answer List 2, for **3** on Answer List 3, and for **4** on Answer list 4.

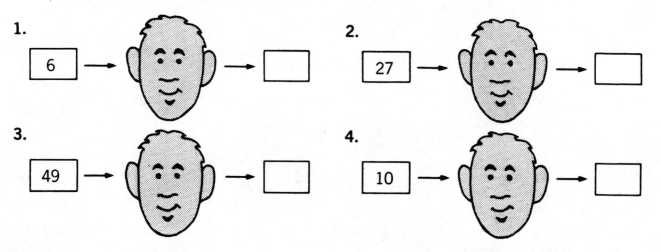

1. 6 →

2. 27 →

3. 49 →

4. 10 →

The answer to **4** is the height in meters of the world's tallest rocket (Saturn V).

30

What's My Rule?

4 → 13

The "out" numbers are almost multiples of what number?

10 → 31

2 → 7

Try to guess what number comes out. If you need a hint, look up the answer for **1** on Answer List 1, for **2** on Answer List 2, for **3** on Answer List 3, and for **4** on Answer list 4.

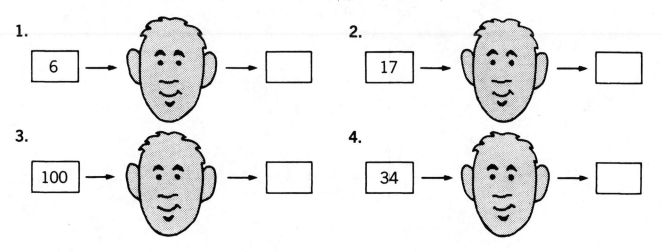

1. 6 →

2. 17 →

3. 100 →

4. 34 →

The answer to **4** is the length in decimeters of the longest feather (of an onagadori cock).

What's My Rule?

$2 \rightarrow$ [face] $\rightarrow 13$

The "out" numbers are almost multiples of what number?

$9 \rightarrow$ [face] $\rightarrow 48$

$5 \rightarrow$ [face] $\rightarrow 28$

Try to guess what number comes out. If you need a hint, look up the answer for **1** on Answer List 1, for **2** on Answer List 2, for **3** on Answer List 3, and for **4** on Answer list 4.

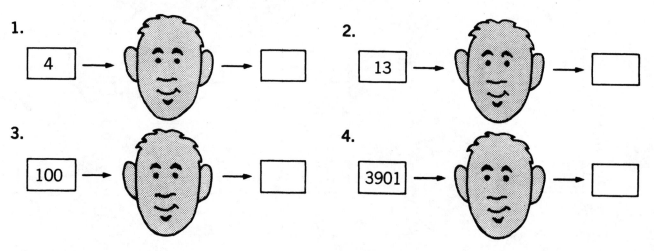

1. $4 \rightarrow$ [face] $\rightarrow$ [ ]

2. $13 \rightarrow$ [face] $\rightarrow$ [ ]

3. $100 \rightarrow$ [face] $\rightarrow$ [ ]

4. $3901 \rightarrow$ [face] $\rightarrow$ [ ]

The answer to **4** is the weight in grams of the heaviest coin (a Swedish 10-daler piece).

32

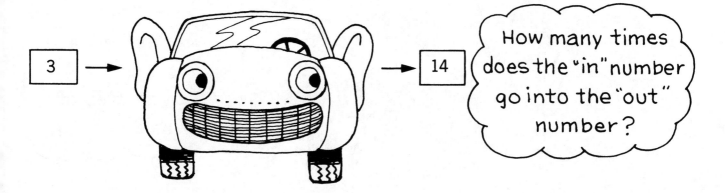

3 → [car] → 14

How many times does the "in" number go into the "out" number?

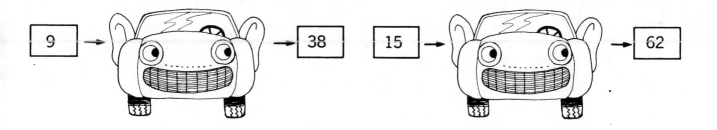

9 → [car] → 38

15 → [car] → 62

Try to guess what number comes out. If you need a hint, look up the answer for **1** on Answer List 1, for **2** on Answer List 2, for **3** on Answer List 3, and for **4** on Answer list 4.

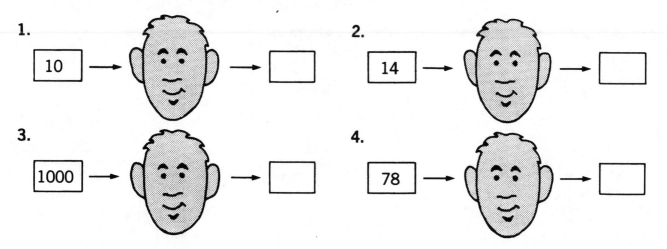

1. 10 → [face] → □

2. 14 → [face] → □

3. 1000 → [face] → □

4. 78 → [face] → □

The answer to **4** is the speed in kilometers per hour of the fastest road car.

What's My Rule?

3 → 14

The "out" numbers are almost multiples of what number?

8 → 39   16 → 79

Try to guess what number comes out. If you need a hint, look up the answer for **1** on Answer List 1, for **2** on Answer List 2, for **3** on Answer List 3, and for **4** on Answer list 4.

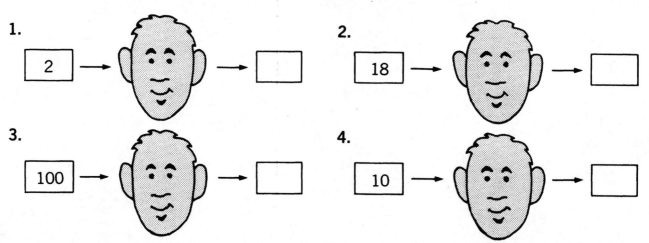

1. 2 →

2. 18 →

3. 100 →

4. 10 →

The answer to **4** is the age in centuries of the oldest tree (a bristlecone pine).

What's My Rule?

3 → 25

9 → 79

20 → 178

Try to guess what number comes out. If you need a hint, look up the answer for **1** on Answer List 1, for **2** on Answer List 2, for **3** on Answer List 3, and for **4** on Answer list 4.

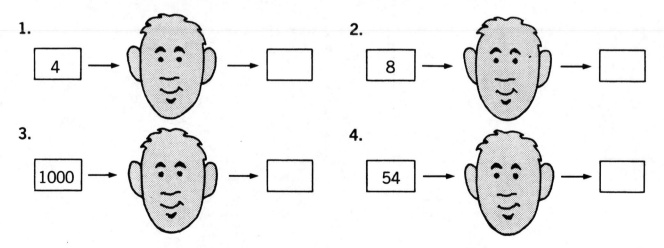

1. 4 → □

2. 8 → □

3. 1000 → □

4. 54 → □

The answer to **4** is the weight in kilograms of the heaviest man that ever lived.

What's My Rule?

3 → 24

8 → 74   11 → 104

Try to guess what number comes out. If you need a hint, look up the answer for **1** on Answer List 1, for **2** on Answer List 2, for **3** on Answer List 3, and for **4** on Answer list 4.

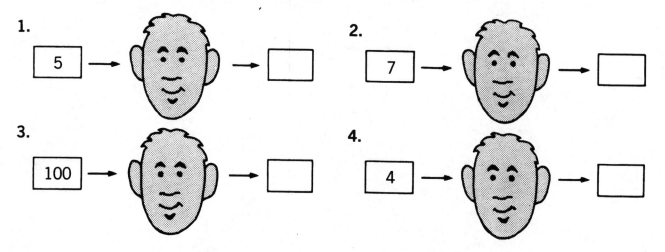

1. 5 →

2. 7 →

3. 100 →

4. 4 →

The answer to **4** is the average temperature in degrees Celsius of the hottest place in the world (in Ethiopia).

What's My Rule?

What's special about the "in" numbers here?

Try to guess what number comes out. If you need a hint, look up the answer for **1** on Answer List 1, for **2** on Answer List 2, for **3** on Answer List 3, and for **4** on Answer list 4.

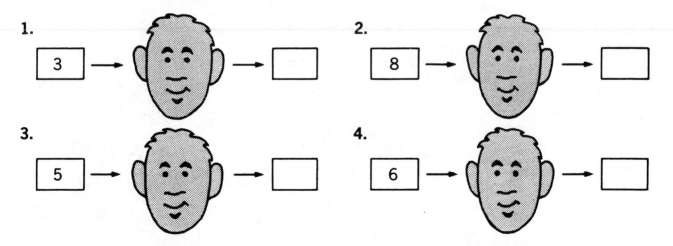

1. 3 →

2. 8 →

3. 5 →

4. 6 →

The answer to **4** is equal to both the sum and the product of the same three numbers.

What's My Rule?

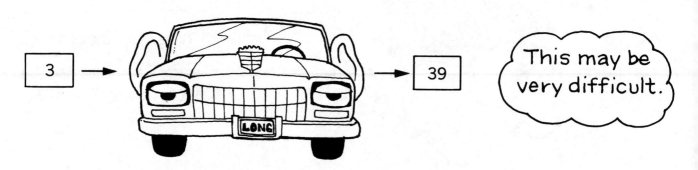

3 → → 39

This may be very difficult.

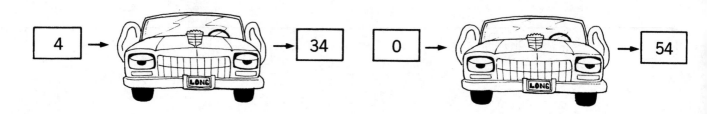

4 → 34   0 → 54

Try to guess what number comes out. If you need a hint, look up the answer for **1** on Answer List 1, for **2** on Answer List 2, for **3** on Answer List 3, and for **4** on Answer list 4.

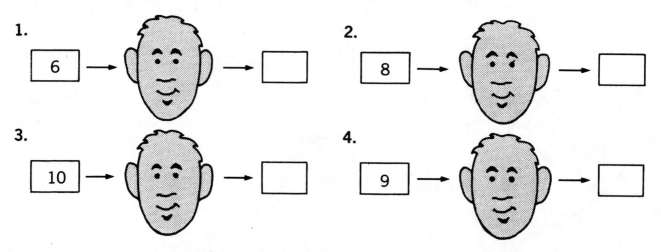

1. 6 →

2. 8 →

3. 10 →

4. 9 →

The answer to **4** is the length in meters of the longest car (a Cadillac).

What's My Rule?

Activity 21

3 → 974

What's special about the "in" numbers here?

13 → 884   23 → 794

Try to guess what number comes out. If you need a hint, look up the answer for **1** on Answer List 1, for **2** on Answer List 2, for **3** on Answer List 3, and for **4** on Answer list 4.

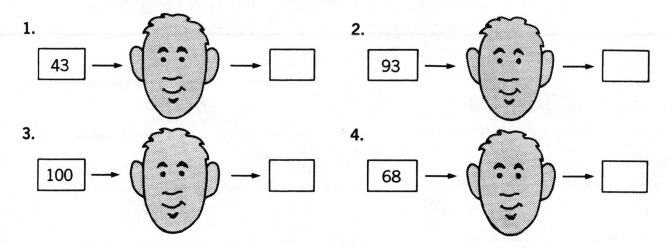

1.   43 → ☐

2.   93 → ☐

3.   100 → ☐

4.   68 → ☐

The answer to **4** is the weight in kilograms of the heaviest Indian tiger.

What's My Rule?

1. 3→☐→39,   8→☐→104,   11→☐→143,   100→☐→ _____

2. 5→☐→13,   11→☐→ 19,   37→☐→ 45,   1000→☐→ _____

3. 9→☐→ 6,   14→☐→ 11,   98→☐→ 95,   800→☐→ _____

4. 5→☐→14,   12→☐→ 7,   2→☐→ 17,   19→☐→ _____

5. 3→☐→13,   9→☐→ 37,   15→☐→ 61,   100→☐→ _____

6. 1→☐→10,   6→☐→ 0,   4→☐→ 4,   5→☐→ _____

7. 4→☐→17,   8→☐→ 37,   17→☐→ 82,   400→☐→ _____

8. 3→☐→21,   13→☐→ 91,   23→☐→161,   103→☐→ _____

9. 8→☐→46,   2→☐→ 10,   14→☐→ 82,   50→☐→ _____

10. 3→☐→34,   18→☐→ 19,   23→☐→ 14,   30→☐→ _____

11. 5→☐→14,   8→☐→ 23,   10→☐→ 29,   1000→☐→ _____

12. 1→☐→87,   7→☐→ 69,   15→☐→ 45,   20→☐→ _____

13. 2→☐→29,   8→☐→ 77,   10→☐→ 93,   500→☐→ _____

14. 0→☐→58,   9→☐→ 49,   45→☐→ 13,   50→☐→ _____

15. 5→☐→15,   2→☐→ 9,   17→☐→ 39,   500→☐→ _____

16. 4→☐→ 3,   11→☐→ 31,   20→☐→ 67,   1010→☐→ _____

To check your answers, use the Answer List for Review Problems.

40

What Comes Out?

Try to guess what number comes out. If you need a hint, look up the answer for **1** on Answer List 1, for **2** on Answer List 2, for **3** on Answer List 3, and for **4** on Answer list 4.

1. In: 3

Out:

2. In: 9

Out:

3. In: 15

Out:

4. In: n

Out:

The answer to **4** is an expression involving n.

What Comes Out?

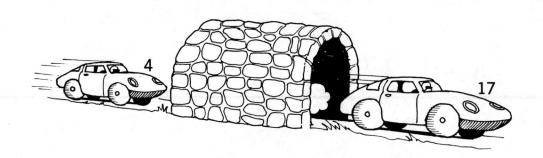

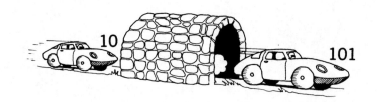

Try to guess what number comes out. If you need a hint, look up the answer for **1** on Answer List 1, for **2** on Answer List 2, for **3** on Answer List 3, and for **4** on Answer list 4.

1. In: 5

    Out:

2. In: 12

    Out:

3. In: 25

    Out:

4. In: n

    Out:

The answer to **4** is an expression involving n.

What Comes Out?

Try to guess what number comes out. If you need a hint, look up the answer for **1** on Answer List 1, for **2** on Answer List 2, for **3** on Answer List 3, and for **4** on Answer list 4.

1. In: 5

Out:

2. In: 10

Out:

3. In: 17

Out:

4. In: *n*

Out:

The answer to **4** is an expression involving *n*.

What Comes Out?

Try to guess what number comes out. If you need a hint, look up the answer for **1** on Answer List 1, for **2** on Answer List 2, for **3** on Answer List 3, and for **4** on Answer list 4.

1. In: 3

  Out:

2. In: 12

   Out:

3. In: 100

  Out:

4. In: *n*

   Out:

The answer to **4** is an expression involving *n*.

44

What Comes Out?

74 is almost what number?

Try to guess what number comes out. If you need a hint, look up the answer for **1** on Answer List 1, for **2** on Answer List 2, for **3** on Answer List 3, and for **4** on Answer list 4.

1. In: 1

Out:

2. In: 10

Out:

3. In: 35

Out:

4. In: *n*

Out:

The answer to **4** is an expression involving *n*.

Try to guess what number comes out. If you need a hint, look up the answer for **1** on Answer List 1, for **2** on Answer List 2, for **3** on Answer List 3, and for **4** on Answer list 4.

1. In: 1

Out:

2. In: 0

Out:

3. In: 3

Out:

4. In: *n*

Out:

The answer to **4** is an expression involving *n*.

What Comes Out?

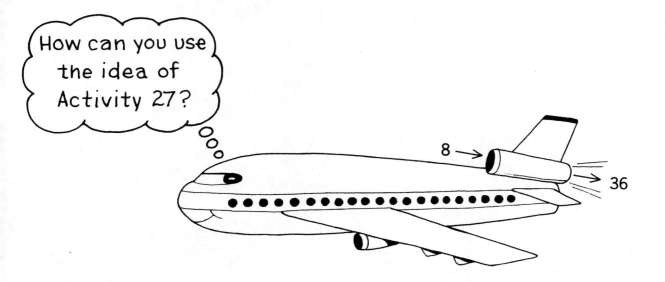

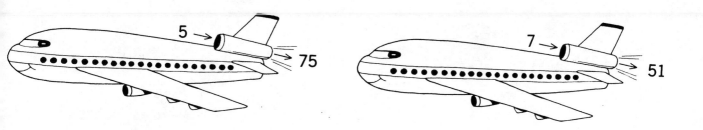

Try to guess what number comes out. If you need a hint, look up the answer for **1** on Answer List 1, for **2** on Answer List 2, for **3** on Answer List 3, and for **4** on Answer list 4.

1. In: 9

Out:

2. In: 2

Out:

3. In: 4

Out:

4. In: n

Out:

The answer to **4** is an expression involving n.

Try to guess what number comes out. If you need a hint, look up the answer for **1** on Answer List 1, for **2** on Answer List 2, for **3** on Answer List 3, and for **4** on Answer list 4.

1. In: 11

     Out:

2. In: 7

     Out:

3. In: 9

     Out:

4. In: n

     Out:

The answer to **4** is an expression involving n.

What Comes Out?

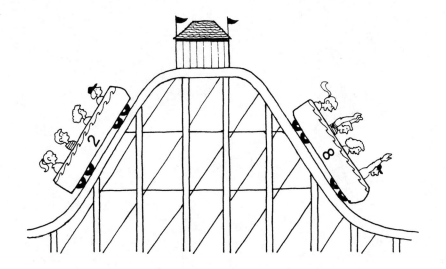

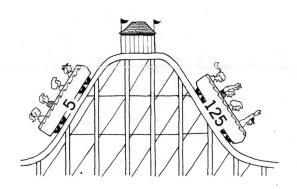

Try to guess what number comes out. If you need a hint, look up the answer for **1** on Answer List 1, for **2** on Answer List 2, for **3** on Answer List 3, and for **4** on Answer list 4.

1. In: 1

Out:

2. In: 4

Out:

3. In: 10

Out:

4. In: n

Out:

The answer to **4** is an expression involving n.

What Comes Out?

Try to guess what number comes out. If you need a hint, look up the answer for **1** on Answer List 1, for **2** on Answer List 2, for **3** on Answer List 3, and for **4** on Answer list 4.

1. In: 6

Out:

2. In: 7

Out:

3. In: 11

Out:

4. In: n

Out:

The answer to **4** is an expression involving n.

What Comes Out?

Try to guess what number comes out. If you need a hint, look
up the answer for **1** on Answer List 1, for **2** on Answer List 2,
for **3** on Answer List 3, and for **4** on Answer list 4.

1. In: 3

    Out:

2. In: 9

    Out:

3. In: 20

    Out:

4. In: n

    Out:

The answer to **4** is an expression involving n.

What Comes Out?

Try to guess what number comes out. If you need a hint, look up the answer for **1** on Answer List 1, for **2** on Answer List 2, for **3** on Answer List 3, and for **4** on Answer list 4.

1. In: 3

Out:

2. In: 9

Out:

3. In: 20

Out:

4. In: n

Out:

The answer to **4** is a slightly complicated expression involving n.

52

What Comes Out?

Try to guess what number comes out. If you need a hint, look
up the answer for **1** on Answer List 1, for **2** on Answer List 2,
for **3** on Answer List 3, and for **4** on Answer list 4.

1. In: 2

Out:

2. In: 5

Out:

3. In: 11

Out:

4. In: n

Out:

The answer to **4** is an expression involving n.

What Comes Out?

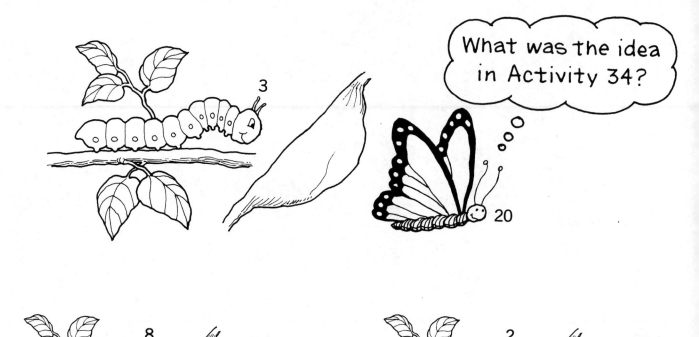

Try to guess what number comes out. If you need a hint, look
up the answer for **1** on Answer List 1, for **2** on Answer List 2,
for **3** on Answer List 3, and for **4** on Answer list 4.

1. In: 10

Out:

2. In: 4

Out:

3. In: 20

Out:

4. In: n

Out:

The answer to **4** is an expression involving n.

What Comes Out?

Try to guess what number comes out. If you need a hint, look up the answer for **1** on Answer List 1, for **2** on Answer List 2, for **3** on Answer List 3, and for **4** on Answer list 4.

1. In: 4

Out:

2. In: 6

Out:

3. In: 1

Out:

4. In: *n*

Out:

The answer to **4** is a slightly complicated expression involving *n*.

54, 128, and 686 are all even numbers. What happens when they are divided by 2?

Try to guess what number comes out. If you need a hint, look up the answer for **1** on Answer List 1, for **2** on Answer List 2, for **3** on Answer List 3, and for **4** on Answer list 4.

1. In: 1

Out:

2. In: 5

Out:

3. In: 21

Out:

4. In: n

Out:

The answer to **4** is an expression involving n.

What Comes Out?

Try to guess what number comes out. If you need a hint, look up the answer for **1** on Answer List 1, for **2** on Answer List 2, for **3** on Answer List 3, and for **4** on Answer list 4.

1. In: 4

Out:

2. In: 11

Out:

3. In: 0

Out:

4. In: n

Out:

The answer to **4** is an expression involving n.

What Comes Out?

Try to guess what number comes out. If you need a hint, look up the answer for **1** on Answer List 1, for **2** on Answer List 2, for **3** on Answer List 3, and for **4** on Answer list 4.

1. In: 2

   Out:

2. In: 3

   Out:

3. In: 9

   Out:

4. In: *n*

   Out:

The answer to **4** is an expression involving *n*.

What Comes Out?

Try to guess what number comes out. If you need a hint, look up the answer for **1** on Answer List 1, for **2** on Answer List 2, for **3** on Answer List 3, and for **4** on Answer list 4.

1. In: 2

Out:

2. In: 1

Out:

3. In: 4

Out:

4. In: n

Out:

The answer to **4** is an expression involving n.

What Comes Out?

Try to guess what number comes out. If you need a hint, look up the answer for **1** on Answer List 1, for **2** on Answer List 2, for **3** on Answer List 3, and for **4** on Answer list 4.

1. In: 2

Out:

2. In: 4

Out:

3. In: 1

Out:

4. In: _n_

Out:

The answer to **4** is an expression involving _n_.

What Comes Out?

Try to guess what number comes out. If you need a hint, look
up the answer for **1** on Answer List 1, for **2** on Answer List 2,
for **3** on Answer List 3, and for **4** on Answer list 4.

1. In: 2

    Out:

2. In: 5

    Out:

3. In: 6

    Out:

4. In: n

    Out:

The answer to **4** is an expression involving n.

What Comes Out?

Try to guess what number comes out. If you need a hint, look up the answer for **1** on Answer List 1, for **2** on Answer List 2, for **3** on Answer List 3, and for **4** on Answer list 4.

1. In: 3

    Out:

2. In: 5

    Out:

3. In: 6

    Out:

4. In: *n*

    Out:

The answer to **4** is an expression involving *n*.

What Comes Out?

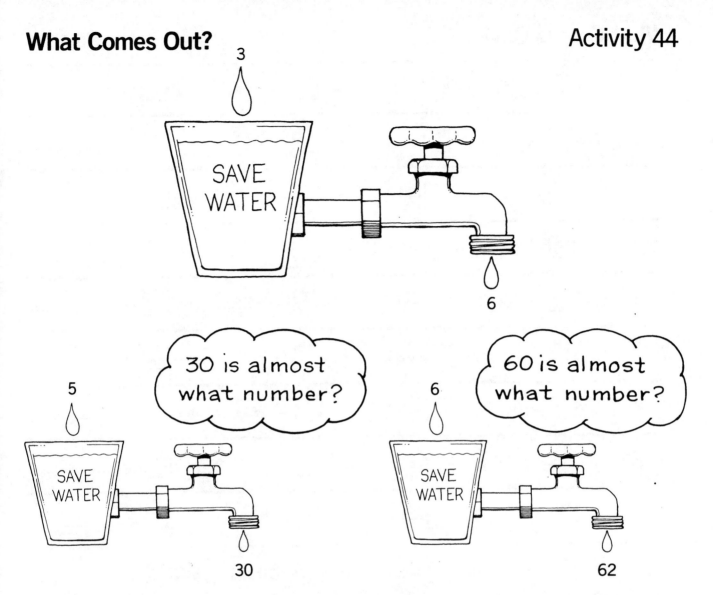

Try to guess what number comes out. If you need a hint, look up the answer for **1** on Answer List 1, for **2** on Answer List 2, for **3** on Answer List 3, and for **4** on Answer list 4.

1. In: 2

Out:

2. In: 1

Out:

3. In: 4

Out:

4. In: n

Out:

The answer to **4** is an expression involving n.

What Comes Out?

1. $0 \rightarrow \square \rightarrow 16$, $16 \rightarrow \square \rightarrow 32$, $8 \rightarrow \square \rightarrow 24$, $n \rightarrow \square \rightarrow$ _____

2. $0 \rightarrow \square \rightarrow 0$, $1 \rightarrow \square \rightarrow 1$, $8 \rightarrow \square \rightarrow 64$, $n \rightarrow \square \rightarrow$ _____

3. $10 \rightarrow \square \rightarrow 1$, $25 \rightarrow \square \rightarrow 16$, $18 \rightarrow \square \rightarrow 9$, $n \rightarrow \square \rightarrow$ _____

4. $1 \rightarrow \square \rightarrow 10$, $2 \rightarrow \square \rightarrow 13$, $3 \rightarrow \square \rightarrow 18$, $n \rightarrow \square \rightarrow$ _____

5. $12 \rightarrow \square \rightarrow 60$, $36 \rightarrow \square \rightarrow 36$, $4 \rightarrow \square \rightarrow 68$, $n \rightarrow \square \rightarrow$ _____

6. $8 \rightarrow \square \rightarrow 8$, $7 \rightarrow \square \rightarrow 23$, $6 \rightarrow \square \rightarrow 36$, $n \rightarrow \square \rightarrow$ _____

7. $8 \rightarrow \square \rightarrow 104$, $7 \rightarrow \square \rightarrow 91$, $0 \rightarrow \square \rightarrow 0$, $n \rightarrow \square \rightarrow$ _____

8. $5 \rightarrow \square \rightarrow 125$, $2 \rightarrow \square \rightarrow 8$, $3 \rightarrow \square \rightarrow 27$, $n \rightarrow \square \rightarrow$ _____

9. $5 \rightarrow \square \rightarrow 27$, $2 \rightarrow \square \rightarrow 12$, $3 \rightarrow \square \rightarrow 17$, $n \rightarrow \square \rightarrow$ _____

10. $1 \rightarrow \square \rightarrow 3$, $4 \rightarrow \square \rightarrow 66$, $10 \rightarrow \square \rightarrow 1002$, $n \rightarrow \square \rightarrow$ _____

11. $1 \rightarrow \square \rightarrow 4$, $4 \rightarrow \square \rightarrow 25$, $9 \rightarrow \square \rightarrow 60$, $n \rightarrow \square \rightarrow$ _____

12. $2 \rightarrow \square \rightarrow 5$, $3 \rightarrow \square \rightarrow 24$, $7 \rightarrow \square \rightarrow 340$, $n \rightarrow \square \rightarrow$ _____

13. $3 \rightarrow \square \rightarrow 91$, $30 \rightarrow \square \rightarrow 10$, $12 \rightarrow \square \rightarrow 64$, $n \rightarrow \square \rightarrow$ _____

14. $3 \rightarrow \square \rightarrow 9$, $1 \rightarrow \square \rightarrow 3$, $2 \rightarrow \square \rightarrow 5$, $n \rightarrow \square \rightarrow$ _____

15. $3 \rightarrow \square \rightarrow 26$, $1 \rightarrow \square \rightarrow 2$, $2 \rightarrow \square \rightarrow 8$, $n \rightarrow \square \rightarrow$ _____

16. $6 \rightarrow \square \rightarrow 36$, $5 \rightarrow \square \rightarrow 68$, $3 \rightarrow \square \rightarrow 92$, $n \rightarrow \square \rightarrow$ _____

To check your answers, use the Answer List for Review Problems.

What Comes Next?

Try to guess what number comes next. If you can't guess,
look up the answer for **1** on Answer List 1, for **2** on Answer
List 2, and for **3** on Answer List 3.

1.   **2.**   **3.**

4. So far, we have pictured 8
horses. If we had *n* horses, what
expression involving *n* would go
on the last horse? (You can check
your answer on Answer List 4.)

What Comes Next?

Try to guess what number comes next. If you can't guess, look up the answer for **1** on Answer List 1, for **2** on Answer List 2, and for **3** on Answer List 3.

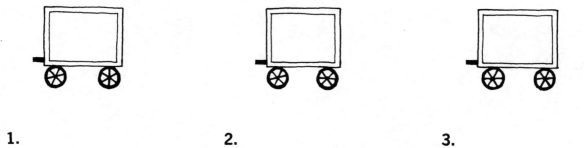

1.

2.

3.

4. So far, we have pictured a train with 8 cars. If the train had *n* cars, what expression involving *n* would go on the last car? (You can check your answer on Answer List 4.)

66

What Comes Next?

Try to guess what number comes next. If you can't guess, look up the answer for **1** on Answer List 1, for **2** on Answer List 2, and for **3** on Answer List 3.

1.　　　　　　　　　**2.**　　　　　　　　　**3.**

4. So far, we have pictured 8 bike riders. If we had *n* riders, what expression involving *n* would go on the sign of the last bike rider? (You can check your answer on Answer List 4.)

What Comes Next?

Try to guess what number comes next. If you can't guess, look up the answer for **1** on Answer List 1, for **2** on Answer List 2, and for **3** on Answer List 3.

1.

2.

3.

4. So far, we have pictured 8 elephants. If we had *n* elephants, what expression involving *n* would go on the last elephant? (You can check your answer on Answer List 4.)

What Comes Next?

Try to guess what number comes next. If you can't guess, look up the answer for **1** on Answer List 1, for **2** on Answer List 2, and for **3** on Answer List 3.

1.   **2.**   **3.**

4. So far, we have pictured 8 airplanes. If we had *n* airplanes, what expression involving *n* would go on the last airplane? (You can check your answer on Answer List 4.)

What Comes Next?

Try to guess what number comes next. If you can't guess, look up the answer for **1** on Answer List 1, for **2** on Answer List 2, and for **3** on Answer List 3.

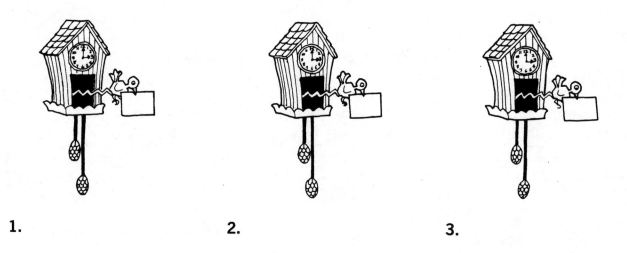

1.

2.

3.

4. So far, we have pictured 8 cuckoo clocks. If we had *n* clocks, what expression involving *n* would be on the sign hanging from the last cuckoo? (You can check your answer on Answer List 4.)

What Comes Next?

Try to guess what number comes next. If you can't guess,
look up the answer for **1** on Answer List 1, for **2** on Answer
List 2, and for **3** on Answer List 3.

1. **2.** **3.**

4. So far, we have pictured 8 racing
cars. If we had n cars, what expression involving n would be on
the side of the last car? (You can
check your answer on Answer
List 4.)

What Comes Next?

Try to guess what number comes next. If you can't guess, look up the answer for **1** on Answer List 1, for **2** on Answer List 2, and for **3** on Answer List 3.

1.

2.

3.

4. So far, we have pictured 8 Teddy bears. If we had *n* Teddy bears, what expression involving *n* would be on the sign of the last bear? (You can check your answer on Answer List 4.)

ANSWER LIST 1

Activity Number	Answer to 1	Activity Number	Answer to 1
1	15	27	29
2	10	28	19
3	20	29	29
4	2	30	1
5	1	31	217
6	21	32	37
7	142	33	30
8	242	34	7
9	80	35	993
10	50	36	48
11	18	37	2
12	66	38	320
13	19	39	39
14	23	40	4
15	42	41	9
16	9	42	16
17	34	43	65
18	44	44	2
19	15	45	217
20	24	46	72
21	614	47	82
22	9	48	1458
23	26	49	432
24	18	50	1298
25	55	51	936
26	11	52	67

ANSWER LIST 2

Activity Number	Answer to 2	Activity Number	Answer to 2
1	8	27	30
2	17	28	96
3	44	29	101
4	32	30	64
5	7	31	344
6	38	32	739
7	82	33	738
8	50	34	124
9	100	35	57
10	20	36	180
11	30	37	250
12	297	38	6655
13	52	39	134
14	68	40	2
15	58	41	81
16	89	42	1024
17	70	43	1025
18	64	44	0
19	0	45	344
20	14	46	98
21	164	47	79
22	81	48	4374
23	145	49	686
24	93	50	2403
25	64	51	872
26	110	52	131

ANSWER LIST 3

Activity Number	Answer to 3	Activity Number	Answer to 3
1	29	27	21
2	46	28	84
3	113	29	69
4	95	30	1000
5	87	31	1332
6	75	32	8010
7	76	33	8020
8	57	34	1330
9	114	35	7993
10	85	36	0
11	111	37	18,522
12	539	38	0
13	301	39	3644
14	503	40	16
15	4002	41	3
16	499	42	4096
17	8998	43	4097
18	994	44	14
19	9	45	513
20	4	46	128
21	101	47	76
22	225	48	13,122
23	626	49	1024
24	282	50	4098
25	152	51	744
26	1235	52	259

ANSWER LIST 4

Activity Number	Answer to 4	General Pattern
1	206	$n + 4$
2	259	$n + 6$
3	304	$n + 13$
4	240,091	$n - 5$
5	979	$n - 13$
6	163	$n - 25$
7	152	$152 - n$
8	196	$250 - n$
9	175	$200 - n$
10	115	$5 \times n = 5n$
11	321	$3 \times n = 3n$
12	110	$11 \times n = 11n$
13	103	$3n + 1$
14	19,508	$5n + 3$
15	314	$4n + 2$
16	49	$5n - 1$
17	484	$9n - 2$
18	34	$10n - 6$
19	6	$24 - 3n$
20	9	$54 - 5n$
21	389	$1001 - 9n$
22	$n \times n = n^2$	
23	$(n \times n) + 1 = n^2 + 1$	
24	$(n \times n) - 7 = n^2 - 7$	
25	$n + 52$	
26	$(n \times n) + 10 = n^2 + 10$	

Activity Number	Answer to 4
27	$30 - n^2$
28	$100 - n^2$
29	$150 - n^2$
30	$n \times n \times n = n^3$
31	$n^3 + 1$
32	$n^3 + 10$
33	$n^3 + n$
34	$n^3 - 1$
35	$n^3 - 7$
36	$n^3 - n^2$
37	$2 \times n^3 = 2n^3$
38	$5n^3$
39	$5n^3 - 1$
40	$2^n = 2 \times 2 \ldots \times 2$
41	3^n
42	4^n
43	$4^n + 1$
44	$2^n - 2$
45	$n^3 + 1$
46	$2n^2$
47	$100 - 3n$
48	2×3^n
49	$2n^3$
50	$n^4 + 2$
51	$1000 - 2^n$
52	$2^n + 3$

ANSWER LIST FOR REVIEW PROBLEMS

Problem Number	What's My Rule? Review 1 Answer	Pattern	What Comes Out? Review 2 Answer
1	1300	$13n$	$n + 16$
6	2	$12 - 2n$	$72 - n^2$
11	2999	$3n - 1$	$7n - 3$
16	4027	$4n - 13$	$100 - 2^n$
2	1008	$n + 8$	n^2
7	1997	$5n - 3$	$13n$
12	30	$90 - 3n$	$n^3 - 3$
3	797	$n - 3$	$n - 9$
8	721	$7n$	n^3
13	4013	$8n + 13$	$100 - 3n$
4	0	$19 - n$	$n^2 + 9$
9	298	$6n - 2$	$5n + 2$
14	8	$58 - n$	$2^n + 1$
5	401	$4n + 1$	$72 - n$
10	7	$37 - n$	$n^3 + 2$
15	1005	$2n + 5$	$3^n - 1$

What's My Rule?

Try to guess what number comes out.

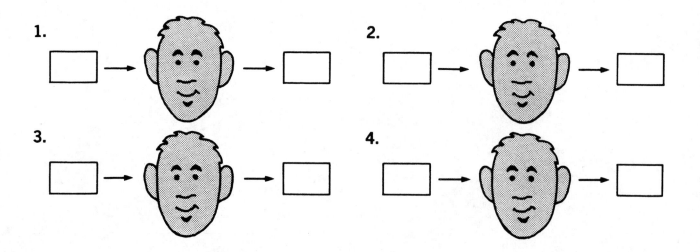

1.

2.

3.

4.

What's My Rule?

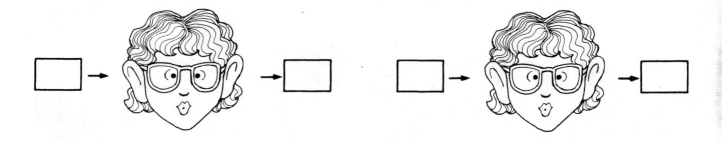

Try to guess what number comes out.

1.

2.

3.

4.

What Comes Out?

Try to guess what number comes out.

1. In:

Out:

2. In:

Out:

3. In:

Out:

4. In: *n*

Out:

The answer to **4** is an expression involving *n*.

What Comes Out?

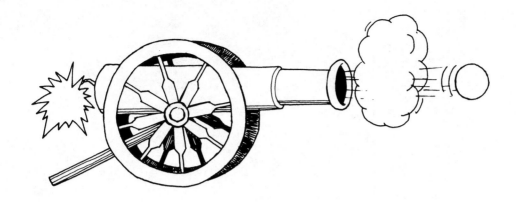

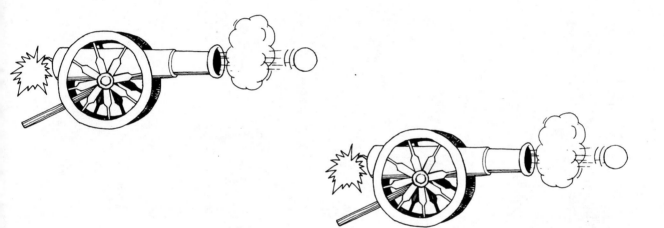

Try to guess what number comes out.

1. In:

Out:

2. In:

Out:

3. In:

Out:

4. In: *n*

Out:

The answer to **4** is an expression involving *n*.

What Comes Out?

Try to guess what number comes out.

1. In:

Out:

2. In:

Out:

3. In:

Out:

4. In: *n*

Out:

The answer to **4** is an expression involving *n*.

82

What Comes Next?

Try to guess what number comes next.

1.

2.

3.

4. So far, we have pictured 8 horses. If we had *n* horses, what expression involving *n* would go on the last horse?

What Comes Next?

Try to guess what number comes next.

1.

2.

3.

4. So far, we have pictured 8
   cuckoo clocks. If we had *n*
   clocks, what expression involving
   n would be on the sign hanging
   from the last cuckoo?